DAILY JOURNAL TO:

GOD SAID IT, NOW WHAT?

HIS DESTINY, YOUR DECISION!

Jeremiah 29:11

Eight Step Process

to Fullfill Your Purpose in the Kingdom of God!

TRACY L. TAYLOR

This daily journal belongs to

Name ______________________________

Address ____________________________

____

____

Published by

JonTra Publishing Company, Inc
P.O Box 2156 Country Club Hills, Illinois 60478-2156
(708) 357-9361
www.jontrapublishinginc.com

Taylor, Tracy L.

God Said It, Now What? His Destiny, Your Decision:

Eight step process to fulfill your purpose in the Kingdom of God/

[Tracy L. Taylor]

ISBN-978-0-9836661-1-0 (Daily Journal)

Book Cover Design: Wendy Russell
Illustration: © Andreus | Dreamstime.com

For speaking engagements, please submit a request by email to:
contactme@tracytaylorministries.org

About the Author

TRACY L. TAYLOR

Tracy L. Taylor is a teacher and an evangelist who enjoy ministering the *Gospel to people. She was born in Illinois* and grew up on the south side of Chicago. As a little girl she had big dreams in making a mark in her world and daring to be different. Through the process of adulthood and life's journey to this point, Tracy has learned significant value of choosing influence over image. She has come to know that she is one of the many someone's who need to do something. This is why for years Tracy has supported and been involved in a wide variety of organizations, ministries and outreach programs which includes mentorship at Indiana Juvenile Girls Correctional Facility, Crisis Pregnancy Center, Light House Missions, Food pantry's for the homeless, Plainfield Re-entry Educational Facility, Indiana Women's Prison and much more.

She is the founder of Tracy Taylor Ministries, based in Illinois. She and her husband, Johnny are the parents of two children: Johnny Taylor, Jr. (son) and Jordan E. Taylor (daughter). They live in Country Club Hills, Illinois.

One of the reasons Tracy has written this book is to inspire people to seek out and unleash their God- given potential. She expresses that the only thing between us and God's plan is our decision. She also realizes that we cannot make the right choice without being properly educated on how to do so. Tracy reveals a much needed message with an eight step process on fulfilling your purpose that will shift anyone into living a life of significance and discovering a kind of success that's ever so satisfying. This book shows that you are one decision away from mediocrity to magnificence!

CONTENTS

INTRODUCTION

Greetings and welcome to the journal portion of *"God's Said It, Now What?"* This daily journal is designed for after having read the book to be used during devotion time so that you may transcribe what God reveals to you through this journey. It is not intended for a stand-alone work book. Each step is structured to help you meditate and study God's Word while you begin your search and proceed towards the process. I pray the book is an effective tool that will help you discover God's purpose for your life and that this journal will record key and vital instructions, revelation, insight and encouraging words spoken or revealed from God to you.

Two things I truly believe is, one, as you seek God and meditate on His Word that you will be given wisdom and sound direction. Secondly, all of what's reveal and is to come that's documented in this journal will not only motivate and propel you but also further encourage and focus you in the distant days ahead. This journal will be as a memorial that will remind you of God's love, His plan and His never-ending faithfulness. God is near and God is fully knowledgeable of where you are and where you are destined to be.

Regardless of how hard difficult is and how impossible the possible may seem, remember God is your strength and your source. My brothers and sisters keep pressing, be strong and encouraged as you fulfill God's purpose for your life. Hardship matures faith! Trust and obey God and do not entertain Satan's fear tactics. When he tries to persuade you that things look very dim or dark, you rest back in faith, laugh out loud; put your hands behind your head while telling him, *"The dark and dim days is where God has done some of His most marvelous works"*! Genesis 1:2 tells us that in the midst of darkness, God created the heavens and the earth.

Adversity should not stop or break your stride but it should motivate and cause you to thrive, feeding your faith. God is your light and dawning of a new day! Do not hide your talent (Matthew 25:25) but maximize the moment and opportunities granted. God has invested in you and He is looking for His return. Today, make the decision that you will no longer be afraid of stepping out and that you're going to enjoy sweet victory one step at a time!

GETTING STARTED

"But the Lord said unto Samuel, Look not at his countenance or on the height of his stature; because I have refused him: for the Lord seeth not as man seeth; for man looketh on the outward appearance, but the Lord looketh on the heart" [I Samuel 16:7] KJV.

Perhaps people do not perceive the potential you have or they might think that you aren't necessary. Maybe you've been pre-judged, overlooked or not included for whatever reason. Regardless of it all, God is aware of how important you are and what great promise you carry. God knows how vital you are to Him and this world. You might ask, *"Why don't people recognize it"* and I would say because of one word called **"perception"**. It is amazing how one person can appear differently to others?

For instance, the above mentioned scripture gives an excellent example of this. The Prophet Samuel was sent to Jesse's home to anoint one of his son's as the next ruler over Israel. Jesse summons all of his sons except his youngest, David. When the eldest, Eliab entered in, Samuel thought surely he was the one but God told him he was not and neither were the others that passed by. Samuel told Jesse that none of them were chosen by God and he asked Jesse if these were all of his sons. Jesse replied, *"No, there's the youngest but he keeps the sheep"*. In spite of the "**but he**" Samuel called for him and it says that when David came in God spoke and told Samuel to arise and anoint him for he was the one.

Here's where perception comes in. When David's family looked at him they only had seen a shepherd boy but when God look upon David He saw a king, mighty warrior, future builder of His Temple and the lineage of the Messiah, Jesus Christ. David's family was limited because they used their insight or intuition thereby judging the exterior where God looks within seeing the heart. Many people have either been guilty of doing the same or have been victim of it. Think of how many people have been overlooked or not considered because of their race, gender or some other unjust reason. Think of how many people who have been disregarded and were the very one who was anointed and chosen by God to do the assignment.

You may have been like David whose family did not recognize his potential and wasn't even considered a candidate worthy to be called in before the Prophet Samuel. Nevertheless, be encouraged because what man doesn't recognize, God will! God knows our giftedness and what it will take to bring it forth. Regardless of who doesn't believe in you, know that God does and He's willing to walk it out with you every step of the way. You may be looking after sheep today but by tomorrow this time you could be overseeing a nation. Imagine that! It's possible! God has anointed you for an assignment so report for duty. Discover or reclaim who you are and unleash the greatness within!

MOMENT OF TRUTH

Of the four pillars called **pay, position, power** or **purpose;** which was the motivation behind the career you are currently in or now seeking? ________________
If your motivation was not for purpose alone then you are setting yourself up for disappointment and statistical enrollment. Did you know according to the U.S. Labor Department, studies show that less than half of Americans (47%) are satisfied with their profession? This tells us that there are a lot of people who are in careers or working jobs that they have absolutely no desire for; 53% to be exact and the number is still increasing!

Just over the last two years I've had numerous of people share with me their discouragement and dissatisfaction with their jobs, careers or professions. All of them were looking for a way out, some were returning to school while others contemplated a mad dash for the door never to look back. Now I'm not saying running back to school is better than running out the door or vice versa, however, what I am advocating is recognizing the signs and heed to the alarm. The important thing here is not how you exit but rather that you exit. You need to get off of the vehicle of nonfulfillment and onto the ride of purpose. You might ask, "How can I get off this train, its moving fast and seem like I'm trapped or going to be on it for a while? First of all, do not panic! That route has a stop or exits approaching and in the meanwhile you get focus so that when your exit comes you can get off knowing where to get on.

As it relates to where you're going, you must first identify the drive within. That inner drive or great desire must be discovered and reveal the purpose of its existence. The reason I say this is because one of the ways of discovering your purpose is by identifying your passion. The two are connected. By no means is ***"passion"*** to be confused with lust. The way to distinguish the two is that passion can't wait to do something while lust can't wait to get something. A more formal definition of passion is ***the object of any strong desire***. It's the one thing you can't imagine not doing while lust is the object of any strong emotional desire being the one thing you can't imagine not getting. Lust is not limited to sexual connotation only. Passion is a strong desire of the heart and lust is a strong desire within the flesh! Passion is also not to be mistaken for fantasy. Fantasy is an imaginative state or illusion of something.

In summation of the three, fantasies are things that you wish to enjoy; lust is things you crave to have and passion is that which you long to do. For truth purposes, fantasy has to be included here for distinguishing and asking of the first question and before doing so, let's establish the importance of answering each question honestly. Please do not deceive yourself! These questions are designed to help you look within and locate where you are so that you can be directed where you need to be. This book and all of its contents are for your eyes only and for the benefit of your growth and development. Take a moment to ponder these questions before you answer them.

What is my passion? ____

____

Is there a connection between what I'm doing now and what I am passionate about? ________
If so, how? ____

____

____

Do I honestly see the two aligned or are they quite the opposite? ________________

____

Finish the sentence:

*If I had to stop all that I am doing right now and from this day forward was only allowed to do one thing for the remaining years of my life, that one thing would be*______________ *because*

____

____

____

Scriptures to study meditate and pray:
Jeremiah 29:11-13, 33:3; Philippians 1:6, 9-10; Colossians 3:16; I Timothy 4:15; Romans 12:1-2; Isaiah 41:10

Study: *the act or process of learning about something; to thoroughly examine a subject.*
Meditate: to think deeply*; to ponder over and over again.*
Pray: *supplication or expression addressed to God; to entreat, ask earnestly or cry out on one's behalf.*

Notes: ____

Before we began individually covering each step, let me first explain the purpose in this segment of the book. The information regarding the steps has been taken from portions of their chapters in the book for the purpose of continued harmony and adequate set-up in further studying, meditation, reflection and prayer. With the wealth of information you have already received in reading the book, this section will allow you to specifically target areas and address anything that must be dealt with. This part also contains a series of questions that you'll need to truthfully answer as well as thoughts you'll need to deeply ponder. Some steps will require you to complete homework assignments that will help you in continued growth and development.

When you look up and read the scriptures that are given, as you study and meditate them, there are also pages where you can write down things that God gives you during this time of engagement within the journal. If you choose to share the contents of your journal or think that you might, still please be truthful and honest and do not hold back what is discovered. It is important that you take your time and allow this journal to impact you in every way. For its intentions are not to shame, disguise, embarrass or belittle but to reveal, correct, rebuild and re-establish God's truth and identity within you. God does not want our problems masked and neither does He want our potential contained so therefore let's get real and let's get going.

Step 1 | PURIFICATION

A Clean Start!

Scripture reference in book {Luke 1:26-27} pg. 152

Purification is cleanliness, being free from sin, guilt and impurities. It also means the act of making oneself clean and pure before God and men. Being cleansed by the "Blood of Jesus Christ" is how we were first made clean but reading God's Word everyday while applying it to our lives and doing what it says is how we stay clean. Just as you daily bathe your body so must you wash your spirit man with the Word of God. If you have decided to make Jesus Lord of your life then you have received God's purification that cleanses your spirit man. Now you must further decide to clean up your natural one.

Question: *What specific area(s) of my life is God showing me that need cleaning up? If there's more than one, list each area separately and then the issues that's revealed.*

___

___

___

___

___

___

___

___

___

___

___

Food for thought! *The only way to get free from the flies, maggots and buzzards of your life is to do away with the stuff that attracts them!*

After reflection, write down any words of encouragement and/or scripture(s) God gives to you: ____________________

In addition to purification, you have to be honest with yourself and admit what you've done, what you're doing or what you have failed to do. The more you attempt to cover it the bigger the mess will become. *"If we confess our sins he is faithful and just to forgive us of them and to cleanse us from all unrighteousness" (I John 1:9).*

Question: *What has God shown me that I've done, am doing or failed to do?*

Food for thought! *The greatest form of deceit is self-deception!*

Scriptures to study meditate and pray:
James 1:6, 13-18 & 20-27; II Timothy 4:12; 5:22; Psalm 24:4

After reflection, write down any words of encouragement and/or scripture(s) God gives to you:

Step 2 | VISITATION

Where are you God, I'm Waiting?

Scripture reference in book {Luke 1:28} pg. 161

As we talk about ***visitation*** please note this word is not used in terms of God going and coming for we know that God is always with us and never will forsake us *(Hebrews 13:5; Matthew 28:20).* This step deals solely with God who is with us revealing His purpose to us. It is important that you understand this because here is where many people end up being impatient and frustrated saying, *"Where are you God, I'm waiting"*? We were on God's schedule the day we were knitted in our mother's womb. God had already scheduled a day of visitation for us all. In the process we must be patience and continue to be obedient.

Question: *What area(s) in my life do I lack patience?*

____

____

____

____

____

____

____

____

Food for thought! *It is not a matter of **"if"** God will speak but rather **"when"**.*

After reflection, write down any words of encouragement and/or scripture(s) God gives to you: ____

____

God disclosed His plan and purpose to Mary and so many others; will He not do the same for you? Begin to pray and ask God to reveal His plan and purpose for your life. As you pray seeking God and He unveils your purpose, be like Mary and respond, *"I am the Lord's servant and be it unto me as you have spoken" [see Luke 1:38].* Do not consider for one moment what people might think or say. I made that same statement and to this day I have absolutely no regrets but certainly many rewards!

Scriptures to study meditate and pray:

- **Patience**: Psalm 27:14, 37:7, 40:1; Hebrews 10:35-37, 12:1; Romans 5:3-5, 8:25; James 1:3-4
- **Finding the Will of God**: James 1:5; Psalm 31:8, 32:8, 119:105, Joshua 1:8, Proverbs 3:5-6, 6:22-23; Isaiah 30:21, 48:17; John16:13

What has God told me regarding my purpose meaning what is my assignment? What gifts has He given me? If He's revealed a vision, then write it down as stated in Habakkuk 2:2-3 and apply your faith towards it. Your life will be a product of your FAITH! God believes in you, do you?

Notes:

Step 3 | DECLARATION
The Power of the Tongue!

Scripture reference in book {Matthew 12:37} pg. 168

Declaration is declaring a proclamation or to pronounce. It's formulating or producing a statement. My declaration is directly plugged into my identification. My identity is my specific person's or state of being. It's who I am. For example, part of my identity is being a female therefore "I am" a woman. Once God reveals *"what it is"* meaning His design or purpose, then at that moment you are educated on *"who you are"*. As you learn *"what it is"* then you can say *"what you are"*.

This part of the process comes by way of the visitation. See the visitation brings forth identification. This is a two-fold in that once God reveals to you what you are to do then you come into the knowledge of who you are. Though this is not the whole of your identity it is a part of it. It's your constituent or *"I am factor"* made known unmasking who you are. Mary was purposed to carry and birth the Messiah which now identifies her as the *"mother of Jesus"*. Her identity was concealed in her purpose.

Many people today, some Christians included have an identity crisis not knowing or being certain of who they are and saying all the wrong things. I am establishes an identity and the identity is made known by whatever follows the "I am". This principle always works regardless if you're making a positive or negative confession. For example, when you declare "I am wealthy" everything that has to do with riches, much money, valuable contents and property assembles itself and begin to magnetize towards you. If you said, "I am broke" then everything to do with lack, poverty, scarcity and insufficiency amasses and rallies itself to be drawn to you.

The universe must accommodate the words that are released from your mouth. You are a speaking spirit who's made in the image of God Almighty *(See Genesis 1:27)*.

Questions: *What negative confession(s) have I been saying or what contradictory statements have I made as it relates to God's spoken Word towards me?* ______________________________

____

____

____

Do I believe what I say or have I developed a habit of saying what I do not mean? ____________

____

Have I been using words carelessly? For example, instead of saying you are excited about going somewhere, in its place you say "that you are dying to go"! ______________________________

What negative thoughts am I entertaining and have failed to pull down (deal with) and take captive (revoke freedom)?

____

____

____

Does anyone else words carry more weight than God's in my life? If so, who and why?

____

____

____

Homework**: Read the entire first Chapter of Genesis. Also for every negative confession, word or phrase that you have spoken, get a scripture to speak in its place and bind the power of those negative statements or words and loose the Word of God over it or them* ***(see Matthew 16:19, 18:18)*! Continue speaking words that line up with God's Words in what He says about you, your children, your situation and entire life. Job 6:25 says, "How forcible are right words"!*

Food for thought: *"If you do not want to see it, then you better not say it"! Everything that God said, He saw (see Genesis 1:31).*

Scriptures to study meditate and pray:

Hebrews 1:3; Isaiah 55:10-11; Matthew 12:36-37; Mark 11:23-24; Romans 8:31; Proverbs 8:6, 10:11, 16:24, 17:27, 18:20-21; Ecclesiastes 8:4; Numbers 30:2; Job 31:30; Psalm 49:3, 141:3; Philippians 4:8-9; Ephesians 4:29

Notes: ____

Step 4 | INCUBATION

The Protection!

Scripture reference in book {Matthew 2:13} pg. 178

The ***Incubation*** is the period of protection and development. This term is not relating to an apparatus but an atmosphere. An atmosphere with the abiding presence of God that provides polishes and protects. The reason you need protection is because you are a seed of purpose that has been planted into the earth by God. Though you have received your design or purpose for the Kingdom of Heaven you still must be trained and instructed by God's Spirit so that you are developed skillfully and will be fully equipped.

You water that seed of purpose and cause it to grow big inside your heart as you read God's Word, obey His instructions and declare His will for your life. In this stage, it's imperative that you consistently filter your life, stay focus and be connected to the right people. You must guard your heart being careful of what you allow into your eyes (**what you see**) and what you allow into your ears (**what you hear**). Satan wants to derail your path, distort your vision and form unholy alliances in your life. **God wants you to soar but Satan wants you to sink!** The things of God will stir you while the things of Satan will stifle you. God wants you stirred so that He may pour out of you what He has poured into you.

Questions: Part (1) *On a daily basis, what do you expose your eyes and ears to? For example, what are you listening to (radio, talk shows, broadcast, music etc.)?* ______________________

____

____

____

____

____

Part (2a) *What relationships exist in your life?* For instance, who's in your social circle and who do you communicate with very often? ______

Part (2b) *Who and what influence you the most?* For example, friends, parents, circumstances, etc. ______

Part (2c) *As a result of this or these relationship(s), how is your life impacted?* ________________

___

___

___

___

___

What areas in your life need developing? ________________

___

___

___

What are the distractions in your life? ________________

___

___

___

Homework: Pray and ask God to speak to you regarding your relationships and reveal anything that He desires to be omitted from your life or daily activity. Wait and thank Him for responding and guiding you in these areas.

Scriptures to study meditate and pray:

- **Relationship/association:** Psalm 1:1-6;, Proverbs 6:27-28; I Corinthians 15:33; II Corinthians 6:14-18
- **Matters of the Heart:** Proverbs 4:23, 23:7; Mark 4:24, Luke 6: 43-45, 8:18
- **Spiritual growth:** I Peter 2:2-3; I Timothy 4:15; II Timothy 2:15; Colossians 1:9-11; Ephesians 3:14-19, 4:14-15; Philippians 1:6, 9-10.
- **God's Protection:** Psalm 91:9-10, 121:7-8, Deuteronomy 33:12; Proverbs 1:33;

After reflection, write down any words of encouragement and/or scripture(s) God gives to you: ______

Step 5 | ISOLATION

A Hiding Place!

Scripture reference in book {Matthew 2:14-23} pg. 186

Isolation is a place of seclusion that temporarily separates or shuts you off from others in which I call the **"hiding place"**. In order for you to be developed you must be placed in an environment where you can be. Also, there are certain things that must occur so that God's spoken Word is fulfilled as said. This applies to you as well in that certain things will happen to get or keep you in the will of God. He is your protector and you have to trust in His protection. You also must trust in His guidance for He is your leader!

It is also within this isolation that you are sheltered by the **"Good Shepherd"**. The word shelter defined is the protection of something from danger or the elements thereof. It also means a covering or place of provision where one receives food and housing. This defines a part of who God is. He's an abiding place that yields protection and shelter to the dweller. Jesus went through the process of seclusion and was briefly isolated for protection, growth and development. He did not ostracize people and become a loner!

As spoken in the book, isolation is not a place of loneliness or abandonment where you have been forsaken; for it is quite the opposite in that you are in constant fellowship with God encountering the richness and abundance of Him. It's intimacy with the Father (***see Chapter 9, pages 168-171***) in means of God doing something within you.

Questions: *How and when do you spend time with God?* ______________________

____

____

____

____

Do you have a prayer life meaning do you spend time in prayer daily communing with God listening and expecting to hear from Him? ______________________________

When you pray, do you allow time for God to speak to you? ______________________________

What has God recently spoken to you during your quiet time? Did He give you a scripture? If so, have you meditated on it and has the Holy Spirit given you revelation from it? If not, be patient, meditate and wait! (You may use the space below to write down whatever God gives you.)

____

____

____

____

____

____

____

____

____

____

____

____

Food for thought: *Your grandest most rewarding pursuit will be in the times when you just sit at your Heavenly Father's feet. For those can be the most intimate moments of your life!*

*"For God alone my soul waits in silence; from Him comes my salvation. He only is my Rock and my Salvation, my Defense and my Fortress, I shall not be greatly moved....My soul, wait upon God and silently submit to Him; for my hope and expectation are from Him. He only is my Rock and my Salvation; He is my Defense and my Fortress, I shall not be moved. With God rest my salvation and my glory; He is my Rock of unyielding strength and impenetrable hardness, and my refuge is God! Trust in, lean on, rely on and have confidence in Him at all times, you people; pour out your hearts before Him. God is a refuge for us (a fortress and a high tower). Selah [pause and calmly think of that]! (**Psalm 62:1-2, 5-8 AMP**.)*

Step 6 | PRESENTATION
Brought Out to Bring Forth!

Scripture reference in book {Luke 2:21-40} pg. 191

Presentation is the act of presenting something. This step deals with the timing of God. This step came as a result of the previous ones. Isolation is not being permanently removed but temporarily and you're only withdrawn for a period of time for the purpose of protection and development. The scripture says, *"On the eighth day,* ***when it was time to circumcise him****, he was named Jesus, the name the angel had given him before he had been conceived.* ***When the time of their purification*** *according to the Law of Moses had been completed, Joseph and Mary took him to Jerusalem* ***to present him*** *to the Lord" [Luke 2:21- 22].* There was a time for Jesus and there's a time for you.

God has fulfilled His Word thus far and does not intend on stopping! When we stand in faith on what God said, then God's integrity is pressed upon and God will have no one to make Him out to be a lie. Romans 3:4 says *"Let God be true, and every man a liar".* God can't lie, it's impossible for Him (Titus 1:2; Hebrews 6:18). God will always do what He said! The thing to take notice of in Luke 2:21-22 is that it states, **"When it was time"** and **"when the time of"**. God's timing is His and it's very important that you do not get into the works of the flesh attempting to bring God's promise to pass yourself. Seek God, do what He says and wait in expectation as you further obey Him.

Food for thought! *Think of God's track record, do we have any reason to doubt Him?*

If you do not know God well enough to agree with this statement then please allow me to share this with you. There is no one on the face of this earth that can say that God has failed them. If they have encountered failure or fruitlessness then I guarantee that it is a result of what they have failed to do and not God. God is true and faith is a producer!

Also for clarification purposes, *"waiting on God"* does not promote physically nor spiritually laziness but it means you rest your hands, your efforts of trying to bring things to pass and you employ your faith. Give your faith the job!

That's what it's there for and it is equipped to do a job well done. Besides your faith can do in 1 minute what your hands can't in a 100 years. Faith in God's Word and obedience to His instructions always brings manifestation. Do **only** what God instructs you to do regarding the matter. Be sure to rest your hands and work your faith!

Food for thought! *God does not need our help but our cooperation.*

Questions: *Am I operating in a spirit of anxiousness?* ________________________________

Am I in step with God or have I gotten ahead of Him? ________________________________

Which of the two are more busy, my hands or my faith? ______________________________

Am I cooperating with God allowing Him to develop, present and position me? ______________

Note: If you answered yes to any of these four questions, repent, turn from following those paths, ask God's forgiveness, receive it and get back in the place of obedience, faith, surrender and patience. Pray this prayer:

Father, in the name of Jesus, forgive me for.....(getting into a spirit of anxiousness, getting ahead of you, not standing in faith, not cooperating with You). Lord, teach me Your paths; lead me in Your truth, for You are the God of my salvation and on You will I wait and confidently trust. Lord You open the doors I need to walk through and close the ones that I don't. Put people in my path that You assigned to assist me and remove those You haven't. Lord I confess that I will not waste Your time neither will I get into the works of the flesh trying to make anything happen on my own. You have my undivided attention and full cooperation. I receive Your grace to leave it alone and I exercise my faith that You will work all things out in accordance to Your divine will and plan in Your perfect timing. I commit to doing my part by trusting and obeying You in all that You've said and will say. I now employ my faith and fire my flesh in Jesus' name, Amen!

Scriptures to meditate:
Romans 4:17-22; Hebrews 6:12, 10:23, 12:1-2; James 1:2-4

After reflection, write down any words of encouragement and/or scripture(s) God gives to you: ____

____

____

____

____

____

____

____

____

____

____

____

____

____

____

____

____

____

"Now to Him Who is able to keep you without stumbling or slipping or falling, and to present [you] unblemished (blameless and faultless) before the presence of His glory in triumphant joy and exultation [with unspeakable, ecstatic delight] Jude 24 AMP.

You are to walk out what God has already worked out! It's a predestined plan according Ephesians 2:10 and also a successful one!

Step 7 | PREPARATATION

The Growth Stage, Getting Equipped!

Scripture reference in book [Luke 2:41-52] pg. 197

Just for a moment, I would like to act as an artist by taking my brush and using an array of words elaborately defining preparation that will paint a graphic picture upon the canvas of your mind. It is very important that you understand the depths and its protocol. Preparation is a subsidiary or derivative of the word incubation. Remember that incubation is used to assist in development and the place of this growth in not within a machine but rather a maintained atmosphere within the Presence of God that invokes learning. So with that being said, please allow my stroking to begin.

Preparation is the act of preparing or being made ready for something. It's being supplied, provided for, stocked, furnished, assembled , put together, dressed, decked, developed, qualified, trained, educated, matured, built-up, manufactured, constructed and equipped with tools, resources, ability, wisdom, knowledge, skill, talent and all wherewithal to do something! What is the something? It's that which God has called, predestined, ordained and purposed you to do. Do you get the picture? Is it colorful enough that you can see what all lies within preparation and how important it is?

Whatever you are called to do you must be prepared to do it. There are no short cuts to success neither is there an escalator or elevator. You must take the stairway patiently and purposely not skipping any steps. The scripture tells us in Luke 2:40 that Jesus developed and grew. He became strong being filled with the grace and wisdom of God. We must be developed for we are not exempt therefore we must permit God to mature, educate and train us. Part of that training will require us to be consistent in reading and meditating God's Word while others warrant us to apply it to our lives, heed and obey His instructions.

The Holy Spirit is the greatest teacher and knows exactly how you learn. God's way of teaching differs from that in which we experienced in the natural. The earthly teachers would give lessons and then test you but God permits the test first to teach us lessons. This is better because the experience and knowledge from that which you encountered stays with you making a greater impression, while the others you soon forget after the test has been taken. It is one thing to be taught on something then tested. It's another to go through something and learn a valuable lesson from the occurrence. Experience always leaves a more lasting impression!

Food for thought! *Consistency is the key to growth and getting results.*

Question: *Where or what in my life needs maturing?* ______________________________

____

____

Are you teachable? (Please circle one): Always Sometimes Depends Not often Never

Count back 3 to 6 months of your life, from then to now would you say you have: (Circle one)
Grown a lot Grown a little Stayed the same Went backwards Feel Stagnated

What area(s) have you grown a lot in? Why? ______________________________

____

____

What area(s) have you grown little in? Why?

____

____

____

What area(s) have you stayed the same in? Why?

____

____

____

What area(s) have you went backwards in? Why?

____

____

What area(s) do you feel stagnated in? Why?

____

____

____

Based on you being teachable will determine if and how you grow. I'm sure that if you look at your areas where you grew the most, the methods or things were different from the areas where you didn't grow much or not at all. The more you feed your spirit man with the Word of God, pray, seek and obey God, you will grow. Now as it relates to the areas of stagnation, remember this one thing, ***CONSISTENCE BREAKS RESISTENCE!*** Containment is of the devil. God wants you to grow and flourish, thriving in life.

I would suggest to you in this same area that you seek God to show you any and all barriers that's hindering your progress. Boundaries do not come from outside of you but rather within you. In the King James Version, the word ***"issues"*** in Proverbs 4:23 is not referring to situations. That word issues is the Hebrew word, "towtsa'ah" (to-tsaw-aw) meaning boundary or borders. So limitations come from within not without. For some of you He might reveal where there's pride, un-forgiveness, fear, doubt, resentment, condemnation (which is a spiritual disease); offense, guilt, jealousy, sin or whatever it may be in your life.

The main thing to know is that it's some type of stronghold that's been formed. A stronghold is a sphere or area of the mind where darkness controls formulating a way of thinking. The stronghold is formed when the individual accepts the lie of the devil. The stronghold(s) stifles a person's maturity leaving them in spiritual retardation. Ultimately a stronghold hinders a person from embracing their identity in Jesus Christ.

Dangerously, strongholds are like mental prisons that keep people captive which explain why emotional and spiritual growth is prevented. They also cause grief to the Holy Spirit; conflict; un-forgiveness; division; bitterness; loss of joy; depression; anxieties; indecisiveness; jealousy; financial chaos; and disorientation spiritually, as well as hopelessness. Overall strongholds can keep a person from fulfilling their God given destiny. Strongholds must be destroyed at the root and simple admittance is not enough.

Pray and ask God to reveal what the problem is and be sure to get scriptures that pertain to the area(s) in which you're shown to reform your mind and build up the truth of God's Word so that you can walk in victory. Remember that until your desire changes; you're only going to encounter freedom to the degree you desire to be free.

Area(s) revealed by God: Be sure to write down an action plan to resolve the issue!

1. Issue:
   Scripture(s):
   Action plan:

2. Issue:
   Scripture(s):
   Action plan:

3. Issue:
   Scripture(s):
   Action plan:

4. Issue:
   Scripture(s):
   Action plan:

5. Issue:
   Scripture(s):
   Action plan:

6. Issue:
   Scripture(s):
   Action plan:

Prayer:

Father in the name of Jesus, I humbly admit of these strongholds and I ask and give you permission to destroy and utterly annihilate (name them). According to Your Word in I John 1:7, I curse them to the root and I declare every stronghold disabled by the Blood of Jesus. I am cleansed and they are incapable of controlling, hindering and obstructing me any longer. In the name of Jesus I bind the hand of the enemy and all of his devices and I loose and receive the delivering power of Jehovah Nissi. I turn my mind, will, spirit, soul and body over to the Holy Spirit that I may walk in complete fullness of God's purpose and destiny. I will not be contained or limited in any area of my life. I am victorious and I will wax greatly being made strong in God. By faith, I will be prepared and thoroughly equipped seizing every opportunity while maximizing my God-given potential in Jesus' name, Amen!

Step 8 | DESTINATION
You Have Arrived!

Scripture reference in book {Luke 3:1-18} pg. 205

This final step is where the fulfillment of God's Word and purpose manifests or begin to come to pass. ***Destination*** is defined as a place, station or area where a person may set out for or be sent to. It is not limited to just one place for there could be various locations within one's destination. Take Joseph for example. On more than one occasion, God gave him a powerful dream that indicated his position of authority.

Some days later the dreamer finds himself thrown into a pit by his brothers who were jealous of him. After being thrown into the deep hole, he was removed by these same brothers who then sold him off as a slave to some traveling merchants. He was sold for twenty pieces of silver to Ishmaelite's. From there Joseph was taken to Egypt where he was sold to Potiphar. Potiphar was a high officer of Pharaoh's and captain of the guards.

Joseph went to work for Potiphar as his slave and improved everything in his home because God was with Joseph and His blessing was upon him. He remained there until Potiphar's wife lied on him accusing his of attempting to rape her when it was her that aggressively attacked him because she was attracted to him, burning with lust. Nevertheless, Joseph was arrested and wrongfully sent to jail. However, in jail God was still with him and he was shown mercy and given favor. Joseph continued to do well and was put in charge serving under the warden handling all affairs of the prison.

While incarcerated, Joseph was given an opportunity to interpret the dreams of Pharaoh's butler and baker who were put there because they had offended him. The interpretations were accurate and happened precisely as Joseph said. Two whole years had passed and Joseph was still in prison. Pharaoh had a dream that none of his magicians or wise men could interpret. The chief butler remembered Joseph and told the Pharaoh about him and they sent immediately for him. Before Joseph went before the Pharaoh he shaved, replaced his clothes and made himself acceptable.

Pharaoh told his dream to Joseph and God gave him the interpretation. From that one encounter, Joseph was put 2nd in command to Pharaoh over all of Egypt which was what his dream had depicted. This meaning his brothers and eventually his father and family would have to come before Joseph to obtain food due to the severe famine in the land *(see Genesis chapter 37-46)*. Joseph had multiple stops going from the pit ending up in the palace. Those mini destinations helped refine and develop his character. They prepared him for his ultimate place of arrival which was not in the pit but in the palace.

Joseph's journey looked rough and so may yours but be encourage. Sometimes the pieces do not seem like they're coming all together and even sometimes it seems as though the dream dies before it lives. Remember as God was with Joseph so is He with you. This is not a time where you give up or faint. It's a time that you become radical standing on the legs of faith declaring **"My God is able!"**

In spite of all that Joseph suffered he maintained a good attitude and forgave all of those who wronged him. This is a critical lesson and one that we must all learn. In Genesis 45:1-8, after Joseph revealed his identity to his brothers, he cried and embraced them and told them not to grieve over what they'd done to him. He encouraged them that it was God's will that he be sent ahead of them to preserve their very lives. He also moved his brothers, father and entire family to Egypt and gave them the best of the land. Wow! Grace covers and love knows no limits!

Another attribute I want to bring out about Joseph besides being forgiving, gracious and merciful is that he was humble. Humility is the anchor that stills your boat from boasting or retaliating towards those who hurt you. Joseph considered not avenging himself even though he had the power to do so. He did not throw in his brother's face how they needed him and neither did he punish them for what they had done to him. Instead he blessed them just as the Word of God says we should do in Matthew 5:44 and Romans 12:14.

In addition to what's already been said, please be mindful, though you arrive, do not think you've arrived meaning you become non-teachable, thinking you've learned it all and there's nothing else that you need to know. Do not become haughty in spirit, arrogant or demeaning to others who may not be where you are and remember not to punish those who have hurt or persecuted you. Humility is vital and love is necessary.

Final Food for thought! *You needed God to get there and you will surely need Him to stay there and advance even further!*

Final Homework!

Get a scripture for each and write the following prayers to confess daily:

- *Thanksgiving (thanking God for His plan and purpose for your life)*
- *Humility (asking God for His help, wisdom and direction)*
- *Love (asking God to forgive and bless those who wrong you)*

Thanksgiving prayer: ____

____

____

____

____

Humility prayer: ____

____

____

____

____

Love prayer: ____

____

____

GLOSSARY

Adversity – a calamity; episodes of misfortune.

Advocate – one who speaks on behalf of another or plead their cause.

Align – to bring into agreement.

Alliance (unholy/satanic) – a union or agreement provoked and sustained by spirits, designed to progress the interest and motives of Satan (the devil).

Annihilate – to destroy completely; blot out and eradicate; demolish or render void.

Anoint – to smear or apply oil upon something; to authorize or set a person apart for a particular work.

Authority - the power or right to command.

Bind – to prohibit or restrain unwelcomed spiritual activity; to constipate or stifle with legal authority.

Blessing – the empowerment of God to prosper; God's immeasurable goodness and favor.

Captive – to confine or keep within bounds.

Circumcise – the action that served as a sign of God's covenant relation to His people which involved the surgical removal of the foreskin of the male sex organ.

Communing– to talk or communicate intimately.

Condemnation –a feeling of guilt and unworthiness leaving one with the thoughts of being unfit for use.

Confession – a creed; an admission of sin or profession of beliefs.

Connotation – to suggest or convey; an indicated meaning.

Constituent – a component part, element or ingredient.

Declare – to authoritatively announce openly or state emphatically.

Desire – to crave, long or hope for; a strong wish.

Destined –intended for or predetermined by fate.

Destiny – something to which a person or thing is destined; a predetermined course of events.

Devotion – an act of prayer or private worship; loyalty or deep affection.

Disorientation - to confuse mentally.

Doubt – a waver in beliefs; to consider unlikely or lack confidence in.

Faint – weak or feeble; cowardly lacking vigor or strength.

Faith – an unquestionably belief in God; complete trust or confidence.

Famine – any acute or extreme scarcity; great shortage.

Favor – endued with grace and goodwill.

Fear – to have a reverent awe of God; an unpleasant or strong emotion caused by expectation of or awareness of danger. More practical definition for this one is **F**alse **E**vidence **A**ppearing **R**eal.

Financial Chaos – extreme disorder occurring in one's financial state or monetary affairs.

Flourish – to grow vigorously or thrive; to prosper or be in a state of continued prosperity.

Forgive – to give up the desire to punish; to pardon or give up resentment against a fault or offense.

Freedom – the state of being free; unrestricted; the ability to act without hindrance or restriction .

Fruitlessness – unsuccessful; without results or failing to produce.

Giftedness – to be talented or have the ability to do something extremely well.

God – The Creator, sustainer and ruler of the universe; the Supreme Being and summation of everything holy, righteous and good.

Grace – God's favor or kindness shown without regard to the worth or merit of the one who receives it and in spite of what that same person deserves.

Grief – an emotion of sorrow; or experience of emotional distress or pain.

Guilt – a strong feeling of self-reproach from believing that one has done wrong.

Hiding Place- a spiritual place of concealment where one is safe and covered from any harm and danger.

Holy Spirit – The Spirit of God; third-Person of the Trinity; Paraclete (one who speaks in favor of, as an intercessor, advocate, or legal assistant; Comforter and Revealer of the Will of God.

Hopelessness – the state of being hopeless; having no expectation of good or success.

Humility – the freedom from arrogance; not proud or haughty.

Identity – the distinguishing character or personality of an individual.

Impenetrable – incapable of being pierced or penetrated.

Indecisiveness - showing indecision; inability to make a decision.

Integrity – honesty; sincerity or adherence to a code of values.

Ishmaelites – descendants of Ismael, who was Abraham's first son.

Jealousy – envious or resentful feelings deriving from the works of the flesh.

Jehovah Nissi – One of the names of God meaning, Yahweh is my banner or my victory banner.

Jesus – The human divine Son of God; Christ the Messiah; High Priest who intercedes for His people at the right hand of God; the Lamb of God who was the atoning sacrifice for mankind sins; logos (the Word) who created all things and became flesh and dwelt among us.

Limitations – anything that impound, restrict, constrain, inhibit, control, confine, and keep down or from.

Lineage (spiritual) – a person's spiritual family that comes not by common ancestors but by way of rebirth.

Loose – the spiritual power to release. If satanic, one can loose demonic spirits from any and all wicked assignments, activities or territory, assigned by Satan (the devil) that goes against the Will of God. If godly, one can loose the things of God that aligns with His Will for His people and purpose in the earth.

Manifest – the actual evidence or results of something believed for.

Meditate – to think deeply; . to ponder over and over again.

Memorial – a monument to keep the memory of.

Merchants - one who's a buyer or seller of good for profit.

Mercy – the aspect of God's love that causes Him to help the miserable and moves Him to forgive the guilty.

Motivate – to stir or compel to do; to boost and encourage.

Offense – a sin or crime; a hurting feeling or something that causes resentment or displeasure.

Ordained – the process of commissioning a Pastor or other officers of the church; to admit to the ministry by virtue of great or supreme authority.

Ostracize - to banish or exclude from a group by common consent; to cast out or expel.

Pay – wages or salary; money made

Persecute – to afflict or trouble constantly so as to injure, harm, wound or distress.

Pillar – a main support or upholding of something.

Position – one's opinion or attitude; the place where one is (location); ranking.

Potential – something that can develop or become actual; existing in possibility; capable or competent of becoming real.

Power – great influence, force or authority; the ability or strength to do.

Pray – to supplication or expression addressed to God; to entreat, ask earnestly or cry out on one's behalf.

Pride – arrogance or conceit; a unduly high opinion of oneself.

Proclamation – an uttered statement; an official public announcement; to declare.

Pull Down – to dismantle or take out forcibly; to exert force so as to change the position or status of something.

Purpose – the object for which something exists or is done; one's sole reason of existence.

Resentment – to feel or display displeasure, hurt or anger over or towards.

Revelation – God's disclosure to mankind of divine truth concerning Himself, His moral standards, and His plan of salvation; revealed knowledge by the Holy Spirit.

Sin – lawlessness or violation of God's will, either by neglecting to do what God's law requires or by doing what it forbids.

Spiritual Abortionist – one who spiritually invades wombs of the spirit in order to terminate life or purpose for that which is divinely planned or destined by God.

Spiritual Incubation – the act of being held in a spiritual location designed to provide the optimal environment or favorable conditions for development.

Stifle – to suppress or hold back; stop.

Stronghold - a place or position of strong and powerful defenses; fortress.

Study – the act or process of learning about something; thorough examination of a subject.

Triumphant – Victorious; successful.

Vision – God's supernatural plans and purposes revealed by way of the Holy Spirit regarding one's life, calling (purpose), assignment, destiny or outcome.

Wax (great) – to greatly increase and grow in size, number, strength, volume or duration; to become gradually full.

Wisdom – the ability to judge correctly and to follow the best course of action, based on the knowledge and understanding given or revealed by God.

www.ingramcontent.com/pod-product-compliance
Lightning Source LLC
LaVergne TN
LVHW080249090426
835508LV00042BA/1499
9780983666110